BOER WA

A History From Beginning to End

Copyright © 2017

Table of Contents

Introduction

Because the victors write the history books, we've called the altercation in South Africa quite simply "The Boer War" for generations – a British designation. But ask someone else and the answer might be different. To the Boers themselves, it was "The Wars of Independence", yet to the politically correct they were the "Anglo-Boer Wars", meant to designate the participants without taking sides. But even each specific conflict has its own name. The First Boer War is also referred to as "The Transvaal War." The Jameson Raid is even questioned whether it's rightly part of the war at all, and the Second Boer War is also called the "Second Anglo-Boer War" as well as the "South African War."

How we name something defines how we look at it. Our goal is to look at all of these events collectively, in an unbiased presentation of facts. Hence this history is more properly titled "The Anglo-Boer Wars: From Beginning to End" and we will refer to the wars themselves with the "Anglo-Boer" designation from this point onward.

But no sooner has the naming conundrum been resolved that we have a new problem in deciding just where the war even began. The tensions between the parties involved go back more than a hundred years. The job of the historian can become muddled when it comes to weeding out the facts and how to present them properly.

Let's start, then, with the founding of South Africa by the Dutch, and work from there.

Chapter One

The Creation of the Boer

"…the Boers of South Africa, regarded themselves as a
chosen people, elect of God, and their God was an awful
Majesty, given to revenge upon His enemies"

—James G. Leyburn, "The Scotch-Irish: A Social History"

The area of what is modern day South Africa wasn't entirely unknown to the Europeans prior to colonization. The Portuguese were familiar with the Cape as far back as the 1480's, though they'd named it *Cabo das Tormentas,* meaning "Cape of Storms." This might give a hint as to why the territory was left alone by traders putting in for supplies, by both Portuguese and later English and Dutch traders. This was probably just as well, as the natives of the region – the Xhosa and Zulu – weren't necessarily welcoming to outsiders.

It wasn't until 1647 that the Dutch became interested in the potential of a colony here, after two sailors from a Dutch East India Company shipwrecked there. While the most that shipwrecked sailors could usually ask was to survive such an experience, these two men actually thrived in the conditions, even able to cultivate their own crops in the months that followed. Their return home was filled with glowing reports of the land, and plans soon followed to place a colony at the Cape to serve passing company ships.

In 1652, under the direction of surgeon Jan Van Riebeek, the first fort was built at what would someday become Cape Town. Within five years, the settlement had grown considerably, aided by the Dutch East India Trading Company, who allotted farms to retired and discharged sailors and soldiers. These individuals were collectively known as the "free burghers".

Problems started almost immediately. The Khoikhoi (called Hottentots by the locals) didn't like how the Dutch pushed east into their territories. Disputes arose over the usual: livestock, land, and ownership, and the rapidly expanding colony was almost immediately put to the test in three small wars, the first in 1659, only 7 years after the initial fort was built. This was followed by another in 1673, despite the fact that the in 1671 the Dutch had purchased land from the Khoikhoi, expanding the settlement outside of the fort and the original establishment. The final of these wars lasted from 1674-1677.

While the Dutch-Khoikhoi wars don't seem overly significant in the grand scheme of things, they go to show that peace was not something the original settlers experienced often, or for any extended periods of time. Further, these wars led to a period of growth for the colony, as the Dutch government began active recruitment of more wealthy farmers and patrons to help establish more stability. By 1690, the burgeoning colony was strengthened by the arrival of over three hundred French Huguenots, something we'll cover shortly.

Going back to the 1660's, it's important to understand that a concurrent tension that was building at this time. Already there were problems between the Dutch and the English. While fighting the natives was something almost to be expected, the constant rivalry between Dutch and English for this same piece of territory would set the stage for the Boer Wars two hundred years down the road. The first rumors of war between the Dutch and English surfaced in 1664. By 1666, the fort at Good Hope had begun a transformation into the Castle of Good Hope, a project that wouldn't be completed until 1679. This was one of five fortifications created solely by the Dutch to protect from what was felt to be an imminent war with England.

That war wouldn't come to be until 1795.

In the meantime, the flavor of the colony was quickly changing. Dutch settlers welcomed the French refugees for many reasons – some agricultural in nature, some religious - but it's important to note that these families brought over one thing that had seriously been lacking up until now: women. The initial settlement hadn't included many women of European descent, and until this influx of newcomers, the locals had taken to marrying half-caste daughters of slaves. Now suddenly there came young families, already married with children. The influence of these families would create a large impact on the creation of the Boer.

A new culture and society began to develop. Vineyards grew, and so did the export of South African wine. But while new blood was welcomed, new ways were not. There would have to be some changes within the colony. By law, schools were to teach in Dutch only, not French, and by a single generation, the French were assimilated into the Dutch language and identity.

Let's take note of some facts for a moment. By the early part of the 17th century, the number of predominantly white colonists numbered between eight and ten thousand. As they began to prosper, they exported wheat, wines, and more notably, cattle. The colony also followed the European policy of owning slaves; by the end of the 18th century, while the numbers of colonists were around 15,000m, there was an equal if not larger number of slaves.

During the 1700s we see how life was for the colonists. If they seemed independent, they quite assuredly were not. Ironically, the "free burghers" were still beholden to the Dutch East India Trading Company, at least in the view of the administration of that company. The Company began to use its influence on the colony, not to curb its development, but to ensure that all profits went to the benefit of the Company, not the colony. To enforce this, the Company closed off free immigration, managed all outside trade, combined all legal and administrative powers under its own governance, and even regulated the kind and amount of crops each farmer was allowed to produce.

This also meant that any free burgher could, at the Company's or Governor's whim, be pressed back into service into the Company. It went even farther than that: the children of the unfortunate man could likewise be pressed into Company service if the offender had angered the Governor or an official.

Keep in mind that the majority of the individuals were not tied the to the land. By the mid 1700's many were raising sheep and cattle, allowing a semi-nomadic ability. They became known as the Trekboers, or "wandering farmers" in Dutch; this would later shortened to just "Boers". These rugged individuals lived in the saddle and faced a a rough and sometimes violent existence, where groups called "commandos" were sent out to raid cattle from nearby tribes.

Individuals as hardy as this couldn't stay under the thumb of another ruler for long. To escape the totalitarianism of the Company, the Boers began to push the boundaries of the colony further north, thinking that distance would be enough to weaken the grip of the company on the colony.

This led to new conflicts with the natives. In 1780, the Boers, in order to avoid the Bantu tribes who were advancing south and west, agreed on a boundary between the two groups, effectively ending the trek away from the Company prosecution.

Then in 1795, the burghers, heavily taxed and without protection from the Bantu, expelled the Company. This became a major factor to the bankruptcy of the Dutch East India Company in that same year.

The Boers, now more independent than ever, set their own brand of frontier justice and self-governance. Racial equality however was not among their tenets, even with the free Khoikhoi, so slavery continued until 1834. Sadly, their independence wasn't as long-lived as that.

Going back to 1795, we see more than just the overthrow of company masters. In Europe, things were in upheaval there too. When Holland fell to France in 1795, British forces representing the Prince of Orange, the Dutch monarch who was in exile in England at the time, arrived to take the colony from the French. Upon arrival, they discovered that the "frontier justice" of the Boers had developed a proclivity towards certain atrocities, such as torture during questioning, which the British quelled immediately. They then set themselves the task of governing the colony, in order to bring it back under some kind of control.

The Dutch declined the offer and, seeing another tyranny, the fierce Boers began a campaign against the British oppressors. Battle commenced near Muizenberg on Sept 1st, 1795. In about two weeks the matter would be over and the Cape of Good hope would remain under British control until 1802, when they returned control to the Dutch. Even that was short-lived though, and the British would take control back in 1804. This would last until the culmination of the Boer Wars a hundred years later.

The Boers were not pleased at the control. When the edict came down to end slavery in 1834, the Boers decided that they'd had enough. The Great Trek ensued, where they quite simply up and left, thinking that distance would solve the problems they'd had with Great Britain. By 1854 they'd established two independent republics of their own, the Orange Free State and the Transvaal, both areas where they could live as they chose, under their own governance. This would last until the nearly the end of the century.

What kind of man does this history produce? Perhaps Sir Arthur Conan Doyle said it best:

Take a community of Dutchmen of the type of those who defended themselves for fifty years against all the power of Spain at a time when Spain was the greatest power in the world. Intermix with them a strain of those inflexible French Huguenots who gave up home and fortune and left their country forever at the time of the revocation of the Edict of Nantes. The product must obviously be one of the most rugged, virile, unconquerable races ever seen upon earth. Take this formidable people and train them for seven generations in constant warfare against savage men and ferocious beasts, in circumstances under which no weakling could survive, place them so that they acquire exceptional skill with weapons and in horsemanship, give them a country which is eminently suited to the tactics of the huntsman, the marksman, and the rider. Then, finally, put a finer temper upon their military qualities by a dour fatalistic Old Testament religion and an ardent and consuming patriotism. Combine all these qualities and all these impulses in one individual, and you have the modern Boer—the most formidable antagonist who ever crossed the path of Imperial Britain. – Sir Arthur Conan Doyle, "The Great Boer War"

Chapter Two

Growing Tensions

"The Kaffirs shall tear us apart, but they shall only do this with English teeth!"

—Piet Joubert

Let's take a minute and go back over some of what we just discussed id in a little finer detail.

For nearly 200 years, the Burghers of Transvaal fought against the natives of the area, other factions and even against each other.

As their weapons advanced from muskets to rifles to machine guns, the Boers began to develop into a unique breed of battle-tested horsemen. Their semi-nomadic lifestyle created men who were as comfortable in the saddle as walking. These were not the simple farmers that they were supposed to be. Perhaps if the British had realized that from the start the conflict would have all gone very differently.

In 1795, when a British force under the command of General Sir James Henry Craig secured Cape Town for the Prince of Orange, The Governor of Cape Town resisted at first. However, under pressure from Holland (which was now under French rule) and the Khoikhoi, who were deserting their former masters and flocking to the banner of the now abolitionist British, he soon capitulated.

The Burghers did not surrender without a fight, however; in 1799 and again in 1801, after armed conflicts with those British forces which had been sent against them, they rose in revolt. The 1803 Peace of Amiens handed the colony over to the Batavian Republic.

The occupation of the Transvaal area was ruinously expensive for the British, and offered little gain. The colony remained Dutch with a minimal British presence. During the eight years of occupation, the British introduced what they saw as much needed reform to the Boer ways of justice. One of the first acts Sir James did upon occupying the area was to abolish the aforementioned torture. However, having English propriety forced upon them did not settle with the fierce and independent descendants of the Dutch.

To top it off, after the Anglo-Zulu wars, the British annexed the Transvaal area, effectively reclaiming the grazing lands of the Boers and putting them again under British rule in 1877 after twenty years of independence.

Sir Theophilus Shepstone, accompanied by 25 mounted policemen, announced the annexation without any immediate opposition. From his point of view, the area was near a state of anarchy. He felt fully justified in this, as he had received a commission to confederate the African colonies as he saw fit.

"Nothing but annexation," wrote Sir Theophilus to the Colonial Office, "will or can save the state, and nothing else can save South Africa from the direst consequences."

Though history has condemned his actions as "premature" and "rash," he too was under some pressure, believing that Germany had planned to annex the area if Britain did not.

The Transvaal was under financial pressure as well. The war with the Pedi in the Northeast and the failure of the Burghers to pay taxes had left them desperate and bankrupt.

Sir Theophilus had set up a sort of self-governing system for the Transvaal, and had that plan been set in motion, it is debatable if the first of the Anglo-Boer Wars would have ever had taken place. But in the end, he remained an administrator to the area, and continued the same governance which had characterized the previous regime he'd just removed.

The Boers weren't pleased. In reaction, they sent a mission to England to express their desire to remain independent, despite Sir Theophilus having found some three thousand individuals to sign a petition stating that those in the Transvaal actually desired British rule. The envoy failed. No one seemed willing to listen.

In 1880, the Boers revolted. In November of that year, a Boer by the name of P. L. Bezuidenhout refused to pay extra fees on a wagon, as he'd "already paid his taxes." The wagon was then confiscated by the British. Not one to back down from a fight, Mr. Bezuidenhout became rather vociferous in his outrage. On the 11th of November of that year, one hundred commandos took the wagon from the bailiff and returned it to its owner.

Now that "passive resistance" was "futile" as reported in a newspaper from the Cape, the strong-minded Burghers gave up the pretense of negotiation and organized into a more active resistance. With wildly fluctuating numbers (and roles), somewhere between 8,000 and 10,000 armed men gathered on December 8th near Krugersdorp, and elected a triumvirate consisting of Paul Kruger, Piet Joubert, and M. W. Pretorius. 10,000 Boers attended the election, the largest gathering of white people that South Africa had ever seen. Five days later, the triumvirate declared Transvaal a free state once again under the name of the South African Republic. Here they raised their own flag, severing all control from the British.

In Potchefstroom, the Burghers organized 7,000 men, strengthened by volunteers from Free States, and faced a force of 180 British soldiers. The resulting siege was a shock to the self-assured English, who had assumed that such disorganized and barbaric farmers would be no match for the much-lauded British army. But the Boers had to their advantage an intimate knowledge of the terrain and the area, were excellent marksmen from their hunter lifestyle, and their clothing blended with the African terrain – something that the famous British "red coats" did not have. In fact, the Boers found them rather easy targets even from a distance, against the backdrop of the dry Transvaal.

This would not end well.

Chapter Three

The First War Commences

"Let no man ever despise the shooting of the Boers, they are strictly marksmen..."

—Unknown

Were the British expecting trouble? Apparently so.

One week after the wagon incident, the British were already mobilizing. On November 18th a company of British soldiers arrived in Potchefstroom from Pretoria under the leadership of Major Thornhill with the goal of arresting the ringleaders of the growing uprising. These were joined two days later by a company from Rustenburg, making a force of 180 troops under the command of Major C. Thornhill, who had orders to construct a fort and "show the flag."

The matter was handled casually. The idea that a show of force would be all it took to restore order seemed to suffice, as the men broke regularly at 1600 hours for "tea and cake." The whole thing smacked of a social affair, right down to the evening dances sponsored by the local ladies, and considered to be very well attended.

Keep in mind that it was during this time that the Boers reclaimed the Transvaal and elected their triumvirate. Perhaps had the British known, they might have hastened their preparations somewhat. Perhaps not, as they still felt they were facing a group of disgruntled farmers.

When Colonel Winsloe assumed command on December 12th, all warnings about an approaching uprising were fairly well ignored. In fact, it was Major Thornhill, riding on the post cart back to Pretoria, who spotted the approaching army and then scurried back to warn the British that attack was imminent. The fort was nowhere near finished. Although some men were placed around the small town, the rest sought refuge in the fort. Soldiers, refugees, and those long-suffering women (who had been keeping the soldiers company, passing time in the singing of songs and socialization) all crammed into the unfinished building, filling it to capacity and then some. There they awaited the enemy attack.

The Siege of Potchefstroom

The next morning, a small patrol of Boers approached the fort, but when the English mounted infantry arrived to determine their intentions, they withdrew while firing. The infantry immediately returned fire, and subsequent shots were heard throughout the small town. That night, artillery men were fired upon, and retaliated by shelling the source of that fire.

On the 18th of December, the British flag at the mayor's office was replaced with a flag of truce. The thatch roof had been set ablaze and the mayor was forced to surrender. The truce lasted from noon to four that afternoon, when the terms of surrender reached the fort and the commander there refused to sanction the terms.

The fort had used the lull, however, to fortify the four-foot high walls with boxes, bales and sacks. Every hole was stuffed with straw or spare clothing. This didn't show the most forethought though, as Boer bullets tore through the barrier and spilled or spoiled the contents of these containers, thereby removing the available supplies to the fort. With water in short supply, things looked dire.

The siege lasted 95 days, the lack of food driving the defenders to surrender. In all there were 24 troops killed. One civilian, a ten-year-old boy who had been trying to escape with a group of women and children, was also slain.

Battle of Bronkhorstspruit

In the meantime, the Boers were busy elsewhere.

On December 29th, 1880, Lieutenant Colonel Anstruther and elements of the 94th regiment marched from Lydenburg to Pretoria, but were stopped at Bronkhorstspruit by Boers who demanded the troops turn around and return. Anstruther refused, and the British column was devastated by rifle fire from the Boer ambush, killing some 155 of the 259 men at the front of the column. The Boers lost only two men, with four others injured. The whole incident lasted only fifteen minutes, and took out most of their officers. This was considered the first major battle of the First Anglo-Boer War, though given the nature of the fighting it was hardly a true battle. The survivors quickly surrendered.

While the Boers laid siege to several other British strongholds, namely Marabastad, Lydenburg, Rustenburg, Standerton, and Wakkerstroom, it was Bronkhorstpruit that distressed Colonel W. Bellairs and moved him into action. In a rather reactionary move, he rounded up the local civilian population, took them from their homes and placed them in two defensible military camps. Here five thousand men, women and children waited to be overrun.

The descending hordes of Boers never materialized, however. The Boer command in Heidelberg instead chose to blockade Pretoria and thus tie up the forces stationed there from assisting in other towns.

Chapter Four

Colley Steps In

"The stain cast on our arms must be quickly effaced and rebellion must be put down..."

—Major General Sir George Pomeroy Colley

Things might have gone differently if orders had been obeyed. But the British High Commissioner for South East Africa, Major General Sir George Pomeroy Colley, wasn't about to sit around and wait for reinforcements. Again, the Boer was vastly underestimated.

Gathering what men he could, Colley marched for the Transvaal, claiming to relieve the British garrisons there.

The Battle of Laing's Nek

Standing with his forces in nearby Natal, Colley sent an ultimatum to the Boer. Upon its rejection, he marched his troops to the Transvaal border. The first camp was about four miles from Laing's Nek, a ridge occupied by Boer forces. In the morning of January 28th, 1881, Colley took his troops to the ridge. He had with him ten foot companies, a company of mounted infantry, and four guns.

Colley turned to face the Boers on his right flank. Unfortunately, this exposed his rear to attack from the Boer on his left. The guns opened up on these, but caused minimal loss to the firmly entrenched Boers. The failed bombardment was followed by an attack from one battalion, which was repulsed with a devastating volley of rifle fire, which killed most of the officers. The attacking British took heavy losses all around before abandoning the charge and retreating to the bottom of the hill.

When the cease-fire sounded at the end of the day, the Boers allowed the British to tend their wounded. Over 198 of the English troops had been killed, with 178 of that number occurring in the attempted attack up the ridge. The Boers, by comparison, had lost only 41 men.

This was perhaps the last time the Boers were this grossly underestimated. Up until this point there had only been sieges and ambushes; Laing's Nek was the first of what the British considered to be a true "battle" between enemy forces. To their surprise, the Boers weren't just a bunch of farmers with a skill for sharpshooting as the British had thought. Instead they were recognized as a force to be reckoned with.

Colley returned to Mount Prospect and awaited reinforcements and orders. Communication with Newcastle, however, was dependent upon a dirt track wending through rough terrain and fording several streams. This rough out-country was travelled with impunity by the Boer, who were familiar with the terrain and conditions. This being the case, the Boer routinely interfered with supplies and messages sent between Newcastle and Mount Prospect.

The Boer also intercepted the slow-moving ambulances bringing wounded soldiers to the more permanent base. Some of the Boer leaders of these raids because to grow bolder, having little to no fear of the British. Their probes went progressively deeper into British territory and the intelligence they gathered on Colley's movements were reported back to the triumvirate.

The Battle of Schuinshoogte

The frustrated Colley, in an attempt of a "show of force", made his move on February 8th, 1881. Giving a mail and ambulance convoy a head start, he provided a strong escort to follow. Especially vulnerable on the route to Newcastle was a hill known as Schuinshoogte, where Colley expected his troop to frighten the Boer and clear interference with his supply line.

Taking command of five companies, four guns, and 38 mounted troops, Colley's plan was to meet another convoy coming from Newcastle to supply Colley's troops and escort them back to the base. Colley set two of the guns and a depleted company of riflemen to guard the return, and then set off to the high ground on the other side of the Ingogo River where it met with the Harte River.

When Schuinshoogte, the high part of the pass, was reached, Colley's troops were fired upon by the Boers.

Colley swung his right flank around parallel to the direction they had just come.

The number of the enemy Colley faced is unclear. The Boers record it as some 200, though Colley himself recorded the number as 1,000. What is clear, however, is that many of the Boer who had been in the attack from the morning left in the afternoon, presumably after expending their ammunition. More replacements came and went throughout the day, while the British were pinned down in the heat.

The Boers, taking advantage of what little cover there was, attempted to flank the English, taking special care to target the artillery. When the guns fired, the Boers would move in and target the gunners with deadly accuracy.

The British Calvary, under the command of Major Brownlow, attempted to drive the enemy off, but the Boer turned their deadly accuracy on the horses and the charge failed. Colley sent a company from the right flank under the command of Captain MacGregor to stave off the attacks on the left flank, but MacGregor was killed and his company destroyed. Five men, one officer and four riflemen, were the only survivors.

The evening rains began as a blessed relief from the relentless sun, but by nightfall the cold and chill seeped into the wounded and claimed more men to sickness. The English left the field under cover of night, losing an additional eight men to the flooded Ingogo River.

Between the dead and the wounded and the drowned, the British forces lost 142 men. The Boers lost eight men, with six more wounded.

Chapter Five

The End of the First War

"Remember Majuba"

—British Slogan, 2ⁿᵈ Anglo-Boer War

February 12ᵗʰ, 1881 finally saw fresh troops for Colley, sent from India. Brigadier General Sir Evelyn Wood extracted a promise from Colley to agree to stay put until these troops arrived at the front.

Colley wasn't to be trusted to keep his word. With complete disregard for his agreement with Wood, he marched out on February 26, 1881 with a small infantry contingent with the intent of engaging the Boer encampment on the far side of Majuba Hill.

With two companies left at the base of Mount Imguela, and two more companies left along the road further on, Colley was left spread thin. He arrived at the top of the Hill with exhausted men who flopped down on the ground to rest, not even bothering to build any kind of fortifications or plan much of any defense.

The Boer looked up, saw the British above them and waited for something to happen.

Then waited some more.

When nothing happened, the Boers looked at each other and started up the hill, leaving the more experienced marksmen behind to cover them as they went. Soon they were moving up from various approaches all around the hill, pausing only to shoot at whatever silhouette appeared against the sky. In no time at all the British were pinned down, and the Boers were fully aware of just how small a group were facing them.

For whatever reason, the British hadn't even managed to take the entire summit. The Boer suddenly had the advantage of high ground, and still Colley did nothing, despite the pleadings of his men to charge.

Unable to take it anymore, the British finally broke and fled back down the hill. The handful that chose to stay and fight were quickly surrounded. They surrendered.

Sir George Colley died in the retreat.

The remaining troops fell back to the positions where Colley had left his men, only to find those forces had already been overwhelmed. Only the heavy guns at the main camp could hold back the Boers at this point. The battle was clearly over.

Casualties was listed at 283 men, almost half of what Colley had taken up Majuba Hill. The Boers had lost only one man, with a handful injured.

The whole thing was a disaster, and clearly showed the British once and for all that their old wartime practices were of no use against the modern weaponry wielded by the Boers. The refusal to adapt to the terrain and to the fighting style of the natives had definitely crippled their ability to fight well in this war.

But this wasn't the only problem that the British faced. The leadership was at fault, and many questions remained. As it turned out, the Battle of Majuba Hill had come after truce negotiations were already underway, having been initiated on February 14th, 1881. Why Colley had refused to wait – or listen to orders – is a mystery.

While some questions can never be answered, the results certainly stand for themselves. When the peace treaty was signed on March 23rd, the British had for the first time since the Revolutionary War found themselves on the losing end of a conflict.

The Boer were awarded self-government in the Transvaal under British suzerainty, leaving them to handle all foreign affairs and matters of tribal relations. This was signed and then ratified October 25th, 1881, after which British troops withdrew. This Pretoria Convention was then superseded by the London Convention two years later, which gave the Boer the same rights.

Things should have been quiet going forward. They might have been, had it not been for the discovery of gold in 1886.

Chapter Six

The Jameson Raid

"I have found out one thing and that is, if you have an idea, and it is a good idea, if you only stick to it you will come out all right."

—Cecil Rhodes

While it's easy to give independence to a country that doesn't have much, it becomes another matter entirely when that perceived wealth changes. In the Transvaal, that came with the realization that there were considerable gold fields in that region.

Don't think about the American Gold Rush when you consider this. Instead of singular nuggets found in mountain streams, there were massive veins of gold running through areas at an even levels - the kind of gold deposits that need to be mined by companies and not individuals - the kind of mining that is going to call in strangers from outside to handle.

Sir Arthur Conan Doyle described it thus:

Managers, engineers, miners, technical experts, and the tradesmen and middlemen who live upon them, these were the Uitlanders, drawn from all the races under the sun, but with the Anglo-Celtic vastly predominant. The best engineers were American, the best miners were Cornish, the best managers were English, the money to run the mines was largely subscribed in England.

The Uitlanders would not be solely represented by these nationalities. Soon Germany and France would have a hand in as well. While both were a perceived threat, it was Germany that complicated things, something we'll discuss shortly.

The miners soon outnumbered the Boers in their own country. The Boers were none too happy with the situation. They would have preferred to keep things the way they were, but everything was changing now – and the Uitlanders, who were being taxed considerably for their presence, were bringing in 7/8s of the country's revenue. Soon they wanted to have a say in the laws of the land. At this point though, they didn't have so much as a vote, much less a voice in how things were done, especially in regards to who their leaders were or how much they were paid.

What defense did the Boer's have in all of this? For one thing, they were afraid that this influx of Englishmen would lead to their becoming a British colony again. The rules designed to keep Uitlanders without representation were designed to keep the power firmly in the hands of the Boers.

But not all was in innocence. Corruption was rampant – especially among government officials. Even schools were scrutinized, and questions raised as to why Uitlander children were getting a far inferior education to that of the native Boers.

The Uitlanders were angry; the Transvaal was heading toward another crisis point.

Concessions were made. Uitlanders were told they could become citizens with full voting rights if they lived in the country for five years, which somehow changed into fourteen years as time went by. The laws kept changing, and the Uitlanders weren't making any progress at all. An uprising became a distinct possibility.

Cecil Rhodes, governor of the Cape, felt there needed to be action, something positive to prevent the coming crisis. His goal was quite simply to unify the Transvaal and Orange Free State under full British rule once again. To that end he came up with a scheme that would allow the Uitlanders to take full control.

Timing would be everything. The plan involved an invasion into the Transvaal at the same time as an uprising of Uitlanders in Johannesburg. The invasion would be led by one Dr. Leander Starr Jameson. If they were successful, the government in the Transvaal would be overthrown, Cecil Rhodes could take over and create this area as a British colony.

Quite simply, they messed up.

December 29th, 1895 a troop consisting mostly of Rhodesian police and a certain amount of recruits crossed the border. Their goal was Johannesburg. Their plan was to cross in secret – but the Boers had known from the moment that they set foot into the country where they were and what they were doing. The invading force pressed hard, but were under constant attack from the Boers. On January 2nd 1896 they stopped at Doornkop, a farm in the Transvaal. Sorely needing rest after almost two-hundred miles' worth of hard riding without sleep, they were only two hours from Johannesburg where they expected reinforcements from the Uitlanders.

Here they found out those reinforcements weren't coming. Trapped with the Boers at their back, and a city closed to them to the front, their only option was to fight.

As expected, the whole thing ended badly, with 65 dead (more than 10% of the invading force). The rest surrendered and were put in the Pretoria jail, later standing trial for an action they thought had been sanctioned by the British government. Jameson himself served a 15 month sentence, and the British wound up paying over one million pounds in reparations.

It must be noted that historians have since debated the involvement of Jameson in this entire matter. The action was said to be "out of character" for him. Had he been a scapegoat in a ploy from someone higher up? Evidence points to British Colonial Secretary Joseph Chamberlain, who had been in approval of sending troops to support an Uitlander uprising. His own actions to cover his tracks afterwards seem suspicious, remaining a mystery to this day More on this in the next chapter.

Regardless of blame, the impact of the entire event was felt immediately. If relations between the British and the Boers had been dicey before, they were downright antagonistic now. Especially when President Kruger of the Transvaal received a telegram from Wilhelm II, giving congratulations and promise of future support should it ever be needed.

This was the final push needed. The British couldn't possibly let such an affront go unanswered. As Jan C. Smuts wrote later, in 1906:

The Jameson Raid was the real declaration of war... And that is so in spite of the four years of truce that followed... [the] aggressors consolidated their alliance... the defenders on the other hand silently and grimly prepared for the inevitable.

Chapter Seven

Stage One: The Boer Offensive

"It is my country that you want."

—Paul Kruger

Let's take a closer look at Joseph Chamberlain.

On July 1ˢᵗ, 1895, Chamberlain was appointed Colonial Secretary. He was determined to unite all of South Africa under the English banner, most especially those parts where lay those rich reserves of gold.

He attempted first to bring the South African president, Paul Kruger, to London to discuss Transvaal matters, but Kruger refused, preferring to keep internal matters internal. Chamberlain's next attempt ended in the Jameson Raid, which only served to increase the tension between South Africa and the Boers.

Chamberlain then sent Sir Alfred Milner to South Africa as a British High Commissioner. He reported back his belief that the Boers were poised to take over the entire country, and that "only war" would prevent that from happening. Milner was known as something of a warmonger, and so Chamberlain's motives were pretty clear here in his appointing of Milner into this position.

It should then come as no surprise that tensions remained high, though the status quo was maintained up until 1898, when police shot and killed an Uitlander named Tom Edgar. The policeman in question claimed it was self-defense, but this incident increased tensions further between the Uitlanders and the Boer.

In May of 1899, a meeting between Milner and President Kruger ended with frustration on both sides. Milner felt that Kruger wasn't giving in to enough of his demands. Kruger refused to bend. This wasn't anything new necessarily, but Chamberlain had been working to gain public support back in England regarding a possible war with the Boer, so that when he asked for troops, he got them. The stage was set.

In September of 1899, Chamberlain demanded full voting rights for the Uitlanders, a move that would eventually spell doom for the Boer culture. On October 9th, 1899, the President of the South African Republic issued an ultimatum giving the British 48 hours to vacate. By this point the British had planted approximately 20,000 soldiers on South African soil with more on the way.

The English government refused the ultimatum. The South African Republic declared war on England.

The Siege of Ladysmith

On October 12th, 12,000 Boers advanced on a reinforced British stronghold in Natal called Ladysmith. Ladysmith had recently taken in 15,000 troops under the command of Sir George White. White was advised to hold his troops back, but deployed them forward at Ladysmith and Dundee.

White split his forces, effectively restricting their movements. They would only be able to concentrate their efforts after fighting two battles at Talana Hill and Elandslaagte. White then ordered his military to capture the Boer artillery, starting the Battle of Ladysmith. The battle was disastrous. The British lost 1,200 men and retreated back into the town of Ladysmith. The Boers followed them and laid siege to the town for 118 days. This was a clear defeat to the British.

Meanwhile, things were getting interesting on the Transvaal border at Mafeking.

The Siege of Mafeking

The forces at Mafeking consisted of about 500 soldiers, 300 men from the local town, a local police force, and a cadet corps of boys from the ages of 12 to 15, all under the command of Colonel Robert Baden-Powell. Interestingly enough, it would be his experiences working with these young people during the battle and all that came afterwards that would later inspire Powell to found the Boy Scouts.

The recruitment of the boys freed fighting men from routine assignments such as messengers. Powell also recruited and armed a black contingent nicknamed the "Black Watch" which was used to guard the perimeter. All in all, there were about 2,000 total men and boys in the Mafeking military.

On October 12ᵗʰ 1899, the day war was declared, the Boers under the direction of General Cronje cut railway and telegraph lines to the region. Four days later, Cronje gave Powell an ultimatum to surrender by 9 AM. Powell ignored the ultimatum and the deadline both.

Even though the town was surrounded by more than 8,000 Boer troops, Powell and his men held out for 217 days, largely due to British deceptions such as laying fake landmines in sight of the enemy and elaborately avoiding non-existent barbed wire.

A Sunday cease-fire was negotiated with Cronje's replacement, General J. P. Snyman, for sports, theatrical productions, and cricket matches. Snyman's rigid religious beliefs were offended at first, but he soon relented and even challenged the defenders to a game.

Half of the besieging force finally left for other battles, but the shelling of Mafeking continued. Aware of the imminent arrival of a relief force on May 12, 1900, two hundred forty Boers slipped through the defenses under the diversion of a feint on the east side of town.

They entered into an area inhabited by the native Afrikaans and set fire to the village, signaling the attack, killing one and capturing 30 others, including the second-in-command.

The native Baralong police had stayed out of the fray when the Boers attacked, but now moved to cut off their escape. Receiving no help from the main body, the attackers were soon isolated and split into three groups.

The first group immediately surrendered. The second escaped. The third held out throughout the day, exchanging fire with the British until nightfall, when they too surrendered.

Mafeking's losses numbered 12 dead and 8 wounded. The Boers lost over 60 men in that raid.

The reaction in Britain was one of elation. The word "Mafeking" even became used as a slang word meaning "to celebrate excessively" for a time.

Yet one more siege would be in the cards for the Boers. Let's travel now to Kimberley, 220 miles to the south.

The Siege of Kimberley

The DeBeers company had long feared an attack on the diamond mines of Kimberley, but such fears fell on deaf ears. William Philip Shreiner, premier of the Cape Colony, saw no reason to arm Kimberley further, calling these fears "groundless." The company, however, had taken such precautions as were available, including an arms depot, a defense plan, and a local defense force set in place.

A subsequent appeal met with some measure of success, and the town was placed under the command of Colonel Robert Kekewich. Kekewich had four companies, 120 police, some 2,000 irregular troops, two machine guns, and some 7-pound guns.

Cecil John Rhodes entered Kimberley as the siege began, narrowly missing capture. Rhodes' involvement in the Jameson raids had made him a liability; the townspeople feared he would antagonize the Boers, and both civilians and military did not want him there. But as founder of DeBeers, he was instrumental in organizing that company's resources. However, Rhodes was notably uncooperative with military authorities.

After several skirmishes, the Boers laid siege to Kimberley on November 7th, 1899. The strategy of the attackers was to wear the town down with shelling and to starve them out. The siege lasted for 124 days. Rhodes viciously condemned the military handling of the siege every step of the way, occasionally leaking military positions and secrets to the press.

The siege ended when General French came galloping in to the rescue with his cavalry. This wasn't a true victory however, as this mad dash across the veldt killed many of the horses, leaving the cavalry severely depleted for future conflicts.

Yet while there had been some success for the British with these sieges, they again faced defeat at Colenso, Magersfontein, and Spionkop, leaving this first stage of the war with the rather unsettled feeling that neither side was clearly winning or losing.

This initial phase of the Second Anglo-Boer War is the only stage where the Boer were clearly on the offensive. Subsequently, they would fight a defensive battle against the British. The problems they would encounter would stem from two distinctive factors, the first being a true lack of real organized objective or goal. Allowing themselves to be drawn into these long drawn-out sieges was not to their advantage, and only tied up men and resources that could have better been used elsewhere.

The second problem came from their guns. The Mausers used by the Boers had been purchased from Germany. A mistake in ammunition choice made them difficult to fire with accuracy. This was an error that could not be rectified, as the British very quickly took control of the waters around South Africa, and successfully maintained this blockade throughout the conflict. While many battles were a clear success for the Boers, they would eventually be out-gunned. This does raise several "what if" questions though regarding how this might have turned out if Germany had been able to take a more active part in the conflict. If the European country had been able to provide the Boers with the proper ammunition they so badly needed, the conflict might have been quite different.

Chapter Eight

Stage Two: The Empire Strikes Back

"As a leader of men in the field he is, I believe, without equal."

—Sir Alfred Milner on Sir Roberts

After several embarrassing and costly defeats at the hands of the Boers, popular opinion in England regarding the war was strained at best. England now took a far more aggressive approach, sending thousands of reinforcements to the beleaguered area. But the most significant change in the way the British military approached the continued threat of the Boers may have been the assignment of Field Marshal Frederick Sleigh Roberts on December 23rd, 1899.

Roberts had distinguished himself in India, even earning a barony, a knighthood, and numerous accolades for bravery and tactical brilliance. Roberts lifted the siege at Kimberley (destroying 500 horses in a single day to do so, it might be noted). He then secured Natal, then pressed his men on through the veldts and into the Orange Free State and the Transvaal.

In June of 1900, the Boer capital of Pretoria fell to Roberts' men. In August, Roberts captured Bergendal. The Boer forces went entirely on the defensive at this point, resorting to guerrilla tactics in order to continue fighting.

The British adapted their tactics as well. As Roberts' men moved through the Transvaal, they started removing the families of the Boers who had voluntarily surrendered. These went willingly, having been told it was for their own protection that they go to the refugee camps, in case of reprisals from the Boers still fighting. This would prove to be a tragic mistake, as we will see later.

Roberts returned to England a hero, having effectively ended the war. He took the title of Earl Roberts after handing off command to Lord Kitchener on December 12th 1900, and would go on to be considered one of Britain's greatest generals.

Chapter Nine

Stage Three: Scorched Earth

"The Boers knew the ire that the fire felt
as it moved svelte like a snake through the veldt.
Nothing concerned had been left unturned
as the baas grasslands burned and burned
and burned."

—Beryl Dov

The war was as good as over, or so they thought back in England with the arrival home of Roberts. The victories had been decisive, and surely all that remained was the cleaning up.

Instead things got very messy.

Kitchener's first action as Roberts' replacement was to expand on the aggressive nature of the actions Roberts had used to end the war.

In a move designed to not only break the spirit of the Boers but also to keep them from being able to re-supply or even find refuge, Kitchener took things even further than his predecessor. He divided the country itself into zones and marked those off in barbed wire, the first steps in what was to become an extremely methodical extermination of the Boers.

Taking his men through the Transvaal and the Orange Free State, Kitchener burned farms, slaughtered livestock, and even salted the very earth so that nothing would ever grow there again. To make matters worse, he took the families of the Boers – the women, the children and any non-combative men - and added them all to the "refugee camps." However, these camps had become something much darker and sinister in the meantime.

The burgeoning population of these camps had created deplorable conditions. The British could not, and did not, supply adequate medical, sanitary, or nutritional requirements for the people held there. These concentration camps became terrible places of death as the inhabitants succumbed to death in droves from basic illness and starvation. The numbers were horrifying. It was bad enough that 177 women and 1,676 men had died in such places, but it was the sheer number of child casualties that were the most heartbreaking. 22,074 children under the age of 16 died in these camps. To many who looked back on this afterwards, this was a crime, not just of humanitarian proportions, but of genocide. The impact was staggering upon future generations of Boers.

A note must be made here. The camps weren't only for Boers – they were also used for the other natives of South Africa that have yet to be discussed.

There has been little mention up until now of the native inhabitants of the area other than in passing. Bare mention of Zulu tribes or even of slaves. The truth was that neither Boer nor Britain had felt comfortable with the idea of arming the natives. The thought of the day was that putting a gun in the hands of a black man would eventually bring out disaster, so both sides for a long time strove to keep these individuals out of the fight completely. As things started to fall apart, more and more blacks joined the fight, mostly on the side of the British. These had joined in hopes of gaining equal rights under British rule.

On the other hand, there were many more blacks who had been servants or slaves of the Boers. These were rounded up, even as the families of the Boers were, but were put in distinctly different camps; even in torturous conditions, there was still segregation. The death toll of these individuals was equally horrifying. While there is no way to figure the numbers accurately, estimates range from 13,000 – 20,000 black Africans who died in concentration camps.

These atrocities did not go unnoticed. A British humanitarian named Emily Hobhouse visited the concentration camps at Bloemfontein in December of 1900 and was horrified at what she'd seen. On her return to England, she made the conditions of the camps very public. The tide of popular opinion now turned against the war.

Outside these camps, the Boers fought doggedly on. Kitchener's scorched earth tactics were taking their toll. In 1902 the Boers were finally forced to surrender, despite the protestations of many who wanted to fight on to the bitter end.

Chapter Ten

The End of the Boer

"The bearer, <prisoner name> has been released from prison of war camp <Camp name> on signing that he acknowledge terms of surrender and becomes a British subject."

—Pledge of Allegiance to Britain following the War

The war finally ended with the signing of the Treaty of Vereeniging on May 31st, 1902. The War had ended with 20,000 British troops and 14,000 Boer dead. More disturbing was the loss of 27,000 white women and children – obvious non-combatants. Also not to be forgotten was the deaths of13,000 – 20,000 blacks, also victims in their own concentration camps.

These numbers alone should have left a bad taste in the mouth of the victors. Add to that the three million pounds sterling to be paid in reparations and for reconstruction, this was not a victory to be proud of for the British.

Popular opinion wasn't exactly siding very strongly with the British either, not in their own country, and certainly not on the world stage. The conditions of the concentration camps had met with condemnation from the world; as a result, relations with other countries were somewhat strained, with many giving England a rather wary eye. This would be one of the contributing factors that would lead to World War I.

The South African Republic and the Orange Free State were both absorbed into the Union of South Africa with the understanding that they would eventually have limited self-government. The day of the Boer was over.

The Boer themselves only accepted the treaty on certain conditions, the first being that South Africa would have self-governance at some point. The other being an alliance against the black South Africans. In no way was equality between races to be part of the package.

When the camps opened up, the Boers were offered a choice. They could go home after signing a paper that declared they would accept the terms of surrender and acknowledge that they were British subjects. Many refused to sign. Those who did sign found that even then they couldn't necessarily return to their homes. The "scorched earth" policy of the British had destroyed their farms, and in many places the earth had been salted, making it unfit to grow anything at all. Many, with their families gone, had truly lost everything in the war; now their only recourse was to either leave the country or join the Uitlanders in the mines.

Also, there were Boers who weren't ready to accept the war was over. These were the "*bittereinders*" who rose up in 1914 to protest serving Britain in WWI against their former allies, the Germans.

As time went by, many Boers who initially left the country at the end of the war returned, though they never did sign the agreement, nor did they ever fully accept the British rule over South Africa.

Today the term "Boer" is still used, though it's dying out in favor of the more common "Afrikaner." Regardless, the Boer still fight to hold onto their history and their identity in this changing world.

Conclusion

The First and Second Anglo-Boer Wars were conflicts that created much controversy on two continents, across many different nationalities of peoples. Defined as an uprising or a fight for freedom depending to who you talk to, there are facts that cannot be denied.

This was an incredible loss of life – and not just the lives of soldiers but of civilians. Perhaps this too was a loss of innocence as well. What had started in America as an uprising against a parent country had now expanded across the seas. The right of the British to colonize was being questioned, as was their methodology in taking other civilizations under their "protective" wing, as it were.

There were many more questions raised in just this conflict alone.

Obviously the British were forced to learn much about modern warfare. Up until the American Revolution, they had held dominance by right of force. The Americans had showed them that Britain wasn't the only nation that was mighty and even to be feared.

Dressing in red coats and standing in long lines was perhaps a rather striking and even somewhat civilized way to fight previously, but in places like the Transvaal, such a move was more suicidal than anything else.

The British were forced to not only learn how to fight against guerrilla tactics, but had to come to learn to use those very ways to their own advantage. Learning from the Boer, they would become better fit to enter into the World Wars that were just around the corner, though this would come at a heavy cost.

World opinion was not with the British at the end of the Anglo-Boer Wars. Perhaps that wasn't as important, as divisiveness at home within their own country was more important; for the first time, the British people were raising hard questions about how the colonies were being handled.

As well they should have - the nature of the concentration camps in South Africa alone was well worth questioning, as were matters such as the Jameson Raid. One must wonder if up until this point the British truly felt that they were truly doing the natives a favor, stepping in and establishing a solid government and guidance as to how to develop and grow. The fact was altruism only lasted until the Transvaal had something truly worthwhile to steal. Was Chamberlain so innocent as he had made out, or had greed infested the powers that be to the point of instigating a raid designed to bring a country firmly into the benevolent hands of the British? Was Jameson a man taking unauthorized action, or a patsy taking a fall for those high enough up to pay for his silence?

That seems harsh and biased, but there are many harsh realities in war, and even more questions left unanswered. The fact remains that even a young Winston Churchill, acting as a war correspondent for the British newspaper The Morning Post, had been prisoner of the Boers at one point and found the situation nothing like how the British were treating the natives of the very country they were fighting in. It was said perhaps best by Michael Davitt:

The Boers have shown far more humanity to their wounded enemies than the English. They also treated their prisoners, especially English officers, with much greater consideration and kindness.

There are indeed things that just don't add up. Was Roberts sending people to refugee camps, or to their deaths? Was the blame for that solely in the hands of his predecessor, or was he somehow responsible for the atrocities that were later recorded?

But the Boers were no saints either. Their attacks and ambushes were equally violent, and innocent women and children died on their watch as well (though perhaps not in the numbers of the camps). They certainly were not treating the Uitlanders fairly, especially in regards to heavy taxation completely without any manner of representation.

So what can we learn from this?

It seems so much of these matters could have been handled differently. By listening to orders. By listening to each other. By honoring treaties and honoring one's word.

Independence would come for South Africa – but only for the white man. For a long time, true freedom would stay out of reach. Some would say that by 1907 the Boers had actually won, when theirs was the largest and most vocal voting population in the new Union of South Africa.

Only time will tell, alongside a careful and thorough study of the past. Such is the nature of history.

Printed in Great Britain
by Amazon